This journal belongs to

Claire Burns

Date

30th August 2014

The Lord's Prayer

Our Father who art in Heaven,
hallowed be Thy name.
Thy Kingdom come. Thy will be done on earth,
as it is in Heaven.
Give us this day our daily bread.
And forgive us our debts,
as we forgive our debtors.
And lead us not into temptation,
but deliver us from evil.
For Thine is the Kingdom,
and the power and the glory for ever.
Amen.

MATTHEW 6:9–13[†]

Ellie Claire™

gift & paper expressions

...inspired by life

*E*ver since Jesus taught His followers to pray two thousand years ago, people and churches everywhere have continued to repeat the words of the Lord's Prayer. And with good reason. The relevance of those beautiful and powerful words transcends tradition, ceremony, or poetic verse.

Through the words Jesus prayed, we are invited to come before the very throne of grace and communicate with God. We find in them a guide to intimacy with the Father and a pattern for effective prayer.

Through each phrase of the prayer, Jesus walks His disciples (all of us who follow Him) through a prayer model that includes worship, surrender, gratitude, forgiveness, protection, and requests. Each section of this journal will focus on one phrase of the Lord's Prayer and its meaning for our prayer lives. Corresponding Scripture and quotations elaborate on the theme for deeper understanding and contemplation.

As you write in this journal, may the words of this well-loved prayer come alive in your heart and lead you into a deeper relationship with your heavenly Father.

*O*pen your hearts to
the love God instills....
God loves you tenderly.
What He gives you is not
to be kept under lock
and key, but to be shared

MOTHER TERESA

*M*y heart is confident in you,
O God; my heart is confident.
No wonder I can sing your praises!...
Your unfailing love is as high
as the heavens. Your faithfulness
reaches to the clouds. Be exalted,
O God, above the highest heavens.
May your glory shine
over all the earth.

PSALM 57:7, 10–11 NLT

*L*ive realistically.
Give generously. Adapt
willingly. Trust fearlessly.
Rejoice daily.

CHARLES SWINDOLL

If you took the love of all the best
mothers and fathers who ever lived
(think about that for a moment)—
all the goodness, kindness, patience,
fidelity, wisdom, tenderness, strength,
and love—and united all those
virtues in one person, that person
would only be a faint shadow of the
love and mercy in the heart of God.

BRENNAN MANNING

Great is his love toward us,
and the faithfulness of the
LORD endures forever.

PSALM 117:2 NIV

God came to us because God wanted to join us on the road, to listen to our story, and to help us realize that we are not walking in circles but moving toward the house of peace and joy.... We are not alone on our journey. The God of love who gave us life sent us [His] only Son to be with us at all times and in all places, so that we never have to feel lost in our struggles but always can trust that God walks with us.

HENRI J. M. NOUWEN

> now therefore that the LORD your God is God; he is the faithful God, keeping his covenant of love to a thousand generations of those who love him and keep his commands.
>
> DEUTERONOMY 7:9 NIV

What matters supremely is not the fact that I know God, but the larger fact which underlies it— the fact that *He knows me*. I am graven on the palms of His hands. I am never out of His mind. All my knowledge of Him depends on His sustained initiative in knowing me. I know Him because He first knew me, and continues to know me.

J. I. PACKER

Let et the beloved of
the LORD rest secure in him,
for he shields him all day long,
and the one the LORD loves
rests between his shoulders.

DEUTERONOMY 33:12 NIV

The height of devotion is reached when reverence and contemplation produce passionate worship, which in turn breaks forth in thanksgiving and praise in word and song.

R. KENT HUGHES

Great is the LORD, and greatly to be praised; and his greatness is unsearchable.

PSALM 145:3 KJV

Prayer is the human response to
the perpetual outpouring of love by
which God lays siege to every soul.
When our reply to God is most
direct of all, it is called adoration.
Adoration is spontaneous yearning
of the heart to worship, honor,
magnify, and bless God.

RICHARD J. FOSTER

You alone are the LORD. You made the heavens…, the earth and all that is on it, the seas and all that is in them. You give life to everything, and the multitudes of heaven worship you.

NEHEMIAH 9:6 NIV

*S*ing a new song to the LORD!...
Each day proclaim the good news
that he saves. Publish his glorious
deeds among the nations. Tell
everyone about the amazing things
he does.... Honor and majesty
surround him; strength and
beauty fill his sanctuary.

PSALM 96:1–3, 6 NLT

For [God] is, indeed, a wonderful Father who longs to pour out His mercy upon us, and whose majesty is so great that He can transform us from deep within.

TERESA OF AVILA

God cares for the world He
created, from the rising of a nation
to the falling of the sparrow.
Everything in the world lies
under the watchful gaze of His
providential eyes, from the
numbering of the days of our life
to the numbering of the hairs on
our head. When we look at the world
from that perspective, it produces
within us a response of reverence.

KEN GIRE

The highest human
happiness is to have
probed what is knowable
and to quietly revere
what is unknowable.

*D*oes not all nature around me praise God? If I were silent, I should be an exception to the universe. Does not the thunder praise Him as it rolls like drums in the march of the God of armies? Do not the mountains praise Him when the woods upon their summits wave in adoration? Does not the lightning write His name in letters of fire? Has not the whole earth a voice? And shall I, can I, silent be?

CHARLES H. SPURGEON

From the tiny birds of the air and from the fragile lilies of the field we learn the same truth...God takes care of His own.... He is moved by our weaknesses. He stands ready to come to our rescue. And at just the right moment He steps in and proves Himself as our faithful heavenly Father.

CHARLES SWINDOLL

It is good to give thanks to the LORD and to sing praises to Your name, O Most High; to declare Your lovingkindness in the morning and Your faithfulness by night.

PSALM 92:1–2 NASB

When the soul finds a home in the heart of God, it has found heaven. When we align ourselves to His will, we become channels between His eternal paradise and the world as we know it. Wading in the stream of His grace, our banks overflow to those around us, bringing heaven to earth.

BARBARA FARMER

Thy Kingdom come. Thy will be done
on earth, as it is in Heaven.

MATTHEW 6:10†

Seek first the Kingdom of God, the will of your heavenly Father.
Spend time listening to His still small voice. Allow the Lord to share His heart and
will for your life, your family, and your circle of influence.

God draws us in by invitation and command to participate in God's working life. We gradually (or suddenly) realize that we are insiders in the most significant action of our time as God establishes His grand rule of love and justice on this earth (as it is in heaven).

EUGENE PETERSON

Do not conform to the pattern of this world, but be transformed by the renewing of your mind. Then you will be able to test and approve what God's will is—his good, pleasing and perfect will.

ROMANS 12:2 NIV

In the beginning, as we are
learning to pray, our will is in a
struggle with God's will. In time,
however, we begin to enter into a
grace-filled releasing of our will
and a flowing into the will
of the Father.

RICHARD J. FOSTER

Prayer is life passionately
wanting, wishing, desiring
God's triumph. Prayer is
life striving and toiling
everywhere and always for
that ultimate victory.

G. CAMPBELL MORGAN

Beloved, I pray that you may prosper in all things and be in health, just as your soul prospers.

3 JOHN 1:2 NKJV

There is an essential connection between experiencing God, loving God, and trusting God. You will trust God only as much as you love Him, and you will love Him to the extent you have touched Him, rather that He has touched you.

BRENNAN MANNING

I live by faith in the
Son of God, who loved me
and gave himself for me.

GALATIANS 2:20 NIV

Recognizing who we are in Christ and aligning our life with God's purpose for us gives a sense of destiny.... It gives form and direction to our life.

JEAN FLEMING

We know that in all things God works for the good of those who love him, who have been called according to his purpose.

ROMANS 8:28 NIV

God has designs on
our future...and He has
designed us for the future.
He has given us something
to do in the future that
no one else can do.

RUTH SENTER

*Live for today but hold
your hands open to tomorrow.
Anticipate the future and its
changes with joy. There is a
seed of God's love in every
event, every circumstance,
every...situation in which
you may find yourself.*

BARBARA JOHNSON

Oh, the depth of the riches both of the wisdom and knowledge of God! How unsearchable are His judgments and His ways past finding out!... For of Him and through Him and to Him are all things, to whom be glory forever. Amen.

ROMANS 11:33, 36 NKJV

*G*od usually answers our prayers so much more according to the measure of His own magnificence than of our asking, that we do not recognize His benefits to be those for which we sought Him.

COVENTRY PATMORE

God's will is determined by His wisdom which always perceives, and His goodness which always embraces, the intrinsically good.

C. S. LEWIS

The LORD says, "I will guide you along the best pathway for your life. I will advise you and watch over you...." Unfailing love surrounds those who trust the LORD.

PSALM 32:8, 10 NLT

Jesus Christ is fully capable of bringing about change unto full restoration. Just as His resurrection power brings new life, His redemption power brings new hope. He is able, for He's more than a Savior! He's your Redeemer.

JACK HAYFORD

Christ's one act of righteousness brings a right relationship with God and new life for everyone.

ROMANS 5:18 NLT

When we allow God the privilege of shaping our lives, we discover new depths of purpose and meaning. What a joyful thought to realize you are a chosen vessel for God—perfectly suited for His use.

JONI EARECKSON TADA

I will remember that when I give Him my heart, God chooses to live within me—body and soul. And I know He really is as close as breathing, His very Spirit inside of me.

I pray that out of his glorious riches he may strengthen you with power through his Spirit in your inner being.

EPHESIANS 3:16 NIV

I know the LORD is always
with me.... No wonder my heart is
glad, and I rejoice.... You will show
me the way of life, granting me the
joy of your presence and the
pleasures of living with you forever.

PSALM 16:8–9, 11 NLT

We encounter God in the ordinariness of life, not in the search for spiritual highs and extraordinary, mystical experiences, but in our simple presence in life.

BRENNAN MANNING

*If each moment is sacred—
a time and place where
we encounter God—
life itself is sacred.*

JEAN M. BLOMQUIST

This is how we experience
his deep and abiding
presence in us: by the
Spirit he gave us.

1 JOHN 3:24 MSG

To You, O LORD, I lift up my
soul. O my God, in You I trust....
Make me know Your ways,
O LORD; teach me Your paths.

PSALM 25:1–2, 4 NASB

*I*ncredible as it may seem, God wants...to be a father to us, to shield us, to protect us, to counsel us, and to guide us in our way through life.

BILLY GRAHAM

*W*hy should we ask God for things when He already knows our needs? The most straightforward answer to this question is simply that God likes to be asked.... The very asking enhances and deepens the relationship.

RICHARD J. FOSTER

Give us this day our daily bread.

MATTHEW 6:11[†]

Ask and you will receive. Your heavenly Father knows your needs and He will provide for them. Ask in faith both for your own needs and those of others. Be specific and be prepared for His blessings.

God wants nothing from us except our needs, and these furnish Him with room to display His bounty when He supplies them freely.... Not what I have, but what I do not have, is the first point of contact between my soul and God.

CHARLES H. SPURGEON

My God is changeless in his love for me, and he will come and help me.

PSALM 59:10 TLB

God is not only the answer
to a thousand needs, He is
the answer to a thousand
wants. He is the fulfillment
of our chief desire in all of life.
For whether or not we've
ever recognized it, what we
desire is unfailing love.

*L*ook at the wildflowers....
If God gives such attention to the
appearance of wildflowers—most
of which are never even seen—
don't you think he'll attend to you,
take pride in you, do his best for you?
What I'm trying to do here is to get
you to relax, to not be so preoccupied
with *getting*, so you can respond to
God's *giving*. People who don't know
God and the way he works fuss over
these things, but you know both
God and how he works. Steep your
life in God-reality, God-initiative,
God-provisions. Don't worry about
missing out. You'll find all your
everyday human concerns
will be met.

MATTHEW 6:25-26, 28-33 MSG

Faith is the bucket of power lowered by the rope of prayer into the well of God's abundance. What we bring up depends upon what we let down. We have every encouragement to use a big bucket.

VIRGINIA WHITMAN

*O*pen your mouth and taste,
open your eyes and see—how good
GOD is. Blessed are you who run
to him. Worship GOD if you
want the best; worship opens doors
to all his goodness.

PSALM 34:8–9 MSG

We walk without fear, full of hope and courage and strength to do His will, waiting for the endless good which He is always giving as fast as He can get us able to take it in.

GEORGE MacDONALD

Knowing God is putting your trust in Him. Trust that He loves you and will provide for your every need. When we know God, we know Him like a personal friend.... God is for us! He will never leave us.

TOM RICHARDS

God will generously provide all you need. Then you will always have everything you need and plenty left over to share with others.

2 CORINTHIANS 9:8 NLT

If we pray for anything according to the will of God, we already have what we pray for the moment we ask it. We do not know exactly when it will arrive; but we...have learned to leave this in His hands, and to live just as happily whether the answer arrives immediately or later.

OLE HALLESBY

Trust is giving up what little I have in strength and power so I can confidently relax in His power and strength.

GLORIA GAITHER

He remembers his covenant forever.... The works of his hands are faithful and just; all his precepts are trustworthy; they are established forever and ever.

PSALM 111:5, 7–8 ESV

GIVE US THIS DAY
OUR DAILY BREAD.

We do not need to search for
heaven, over here or over there,
in order to find our eternal Father.
In fact, we do not even need
to speak out loud, for though we
speak in the smallest whisper or
the most fleeting thought, He is
close enough to hear us.

TERESA OF AVILA

We sometimes fear to bring our troubles to God, because they must seem so small to Him who sits on the circle of the earth. But if they are large enough to concern and endanger our welfare, they are large enough to touch His heart of love.

R. A. TORREY

*L*ive carefree before God;
he is most careful with you.

1 PETER 5:7 MSG

He only is the Maker
of all things near and far;
He paints the wayside flower,
He lights the evening star;
the wind and waves obey Him,
by Him the birds are fed;
much more to us, His children,
He gives our daily bread.

MATTHIAS CLAUDIUS

Tuck [this] thought
into your heart today.
Treasure it. Your Father
God cares about your
daily everythings
that concern you.

KAY ARTHUR

God will supply all your
needs according to
His riches in glory in
Christ Jesus. Now to our
God and Father be the
glory forever and ever.

PHILIPPIANS 4:19–20 NASB

GIVE US THIS DAY
OUR DAILY BREAD.

God is a rich and bountiful Father, and He does not forget His children, nor withhold from them anything which it would be to their advantage to receive.

J. K. MACLEAN

The LORD is my shepherd;
I shall not want.
He makes me lie down
in green pastures. He leads
me beside still waters.
He restores my soul.

PSALM 23: 1–3 ESV

Jesus knows when a request comes to Him from the heart. He has been waiting all along for us to bring our needy selves to Him and receive from Him that eternal water.

DORIS GAILEY

God bless you and utterly satisfy your heart... with Himself.

AMY CARMICHAEL

He is the Source. Of everything. Strength for your day. Wisdom for your task. Comfort for your soul. Grace for your battle. Provision for each need. Understanding for each failure. Assistance for every encounter.

JACK HAYFORD

May the God of hope
fill you with all joy
and peace as you trust
in him, so that you may
overflow with hope by the
power of the Holy Spirit.

ROMANS 15:13 NIV

*D*on't fret or worry. Instead of worrying, pray. Let petitions and praises shape your worries into prayers, letting God know your concerns. Before you know it, a sense of God's wholeness, everything coming together for good, will come and settle you down. It's wonderful what happens when Christ displaces worry at the center of your life.

PHILIPPIANS 4:6–7 MSG

I will let God's peace infuse every part of today. As the chaos swirls and life's demands pull at me on all sides, I will breathe in God's peace that surpasses all understanding.

WENDY MOORE

We can approach God with confidence to ask His forgiveness for anything and everything. Having already paid the ultimate price for our sin, He is willing and able to forgive us. The freedom and release from guilt is life changing!
What's more, when we offer forgiveness to those who offend us, it is also freeing and life changing.

BARBARA FARMER

And forgive us our debts,
as we forgive our debtors.

MATTHEW 6:12[†]

Ask God to forgive you for all your sins. He longs to give you this gift.
In response, offer the same forgiveness toward any who have offended you.
This releases the bitterness and opens the door to your own forgiveness.

*G*ive us grace today, O Lord. Help us to be merciful to those who need mercy. Help us to be kind to those who need kindness. Help us to be gentle with those who need gentleness. Help us to be generous with those who need generosity. Help us to be forgiving to those who ask for forgiveness. Help us to be more like You. Amen.

MARILYN JANSEN

Be kind to one another, tender-hearted, forgiving each other, just as God in Christ also has forgiven you.

EPHESIANS 4:32 NASB

Among the most powerful of human experiences is to give or to receive forgiveness.... Forgiveness is a collapsing into the mystery of God as totally unearned love, unmerited grace. It is the final surrender to the humility and power of a Divine Love and a Divine Lover.

RICHARD ROHR

If we learn how to give of ourselves, to forgive others, and to live with thanksgiving, we need not seek happiness. It will seek us.

As those who have been chosen of God, holy and beloved, put on a heart of compassion, kindness, humility, gentleness and patience; bearing with one another, and forgiving each other.

COLOSSIANS 3:12-13 NASB

Forgive us if this day we have done or said anything to increase the pain of the world. Pardon the unkind word, the impatient gesture, the hard and selfish deed, the failure to show sympathy and kindly help where we had the opportunity, but missed it; and enable us so to live that we may daily do something to lessen the tide of human sorrow, and add to the sum of human happiness.

F. B. MEYER

Just as sin ruled over all people and brought them to death, now God's wonderful grace rules instead, giving us right standing with God and resulting in eternal life through Jesus Christ our Lord.

ROMANS 5:21 NLT

Forgiveness is not acting as if things are just the same as before the offense. We must face the fact that things will never be the same. By the grace of God they can be a thousand times better, but they will never again be the same.

RICHARD J. FOSTER

Forgiveness is as valuable to the one who forgives as to the one forgiven.

MARY WHITCHER

*L*ord, how many times
shall I forgive my brother
or sister who sins against me?
Up to seven times?"
Jesus answered, "I tell you,
not seven times, but
seventy-seven times."

MATTHEW 18:21–22 NIV

He did not retaliate when he was insulted, nor threaten revenge when he suffered. He left his case in the hands of God, who always judges fairly. He personally carried our sins in his body on the cross so that we can be dead to sin and live for what is right. By his wounds you are healed.

1 PETER 2:23–24 NLT

Never were God's arms opened so wide as they were on the Roman cross. One arm extending back into history and the other reaching into the future. An embrace of forgiveness offered for anyone who'll come.

MAX LUCADO

Grace is the dynamic outpouring of God's loving nature that flows into and through creation in an endless self-offering of healing, love, illumination, and reconciliation. It is a gift that we are free to ignore, reject, ask for, or simply accept.

DR. GERALD G. MAY

The LORD is compassionate
and gracious, slow to anger,
abounding in love.

PSALM 103:8 NIV

*N*o offense by another person could possibly equal our guilt before God, yet He has forgiven us; are we not obligated to show the same mercy to others?

DR. JAMES DOBSON

The person who is truly forgiven and knows it, is one who forgives.

D. MARTYN LLOYD-JONES

"When you are praying, first forgive anyone you are holding a grudge against, so that your Father in heaven will forgive your sins, too."

MARK 11:25 NLT

Be merciful, just as your Father is merciful. Do not judge, and you will not be judged. Do not condemn, and you will not be condemned. Forgive, and you will be forgiven. Give, and it will be given to you. A good measure, pressed down, shaken together and running over, will be poured into your lap. For with the measure you use, it will be measured to you.

LUKE 6:36–38 NIV

You, God, are the only one who can measure our differences and properly assess our worth; and...in Your Son we have equal standing, equal opportunity, equal access to acceptance and forgiveness.

ELAINE STEDMAN

*Peacemakers calm the waters,
they don't trouble them.
Peacemakers work hard to keep an
offense from occurring. And if
it has occurred, they strive for
resolution.... Peacemakers generate
more light than heat. Blessed are
such great-hearted souls!*

CHARLES SWINDOLL

*L*ove doesn't require technical training. It isn't qualified by a degree or limited by a job description. Anyone can demonstrate love to anyone else, and since God comforts us in all our troubles, is it asking too much to comfort others in any trouble?

JONI EARECKSON TADA

If I can think of myself as loved, I can love and accept others. If I see myself as forgiven, I can be gracious toward others.

KATHY PEEL

*Above all, love each
other deeply, because
love covers over a
multitude of sins.*

1 PETER 4:8 NIV

AND FORGIVE US OUR DEBTS,
AS WE FORGIVE OUR DEBTORS.

*N*ot merely does God will to guide us by showing us His way;... whatever mistakes we may make, we shall come safely home. Slippings and strayings there will be, no doubt, but the everlasting arms are beneath us; we shall be caught, rescued, restored. This is God's promise; this is how good He is.

J. I. PACKER

*I*n him we have redemption through his blood, the forgiveness of sins, in accordance with the riches of God's grace that he lavished on us.

EPHESIANS 1:7–8 NIV

*G*race comes free of charge to people who do not deserve it and I am one of those people.... Now I am trying in my own small way to pipe the tune of grace. I do so because I know, more surely than I know anything, that any pang of healing or forgiveness or goodness I have ever felt comes solely from the grace of God.

PHILIP YANCEY

If someone falls into sin, forgivingly restore him, saving your critical comments for yourself. You might be needing forgiveness before the day's out. Stoop down and reach out to those who are oppressed. Share their burdens, and so complete Christ's law.

GALATIANS 6:1–3 MSG

*Praise the LORD, O my soul,
and forget not all his benefits—
who forgives all your sins
and heals all your diseases,
who redeems your life from the
pit and crowns you with love and
compassion, who satisfies your
desires with good things so
that your youth is renewed
like the eagle's.*

PSALM 103:2–5 NIV

When we focus on God, the scene changes. He's in control of our lives; nothing lies outside the realm of His redemptive grace. Even when we make mistakes, fail in relationships, or deliberately make bad choices, God can redeem us.

PENELOPE J. STOKES

As a result of grace, we have been saved from sin's penalty. One day we will be saved from sin's presence. In the meantime we are being saved from sin's power.

ALISTAIR BEGG

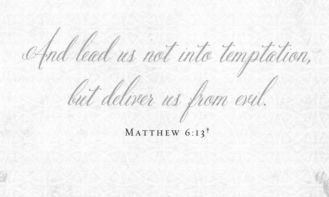

And lead us not into temptation,
but deliver us from evil.

MATTHEW 6:13[†]

God's grace is not only your salvation but also your protection.
Use this gift to stand firm when facing trials and temptations. To resist the enemy,
look to the Lord your deliverer, and He will make a way.

Christ desires to be with you
in whatever crisis you may find
yourself. Call upon His name.
See if He will not do as He
promised He would. He will not
make your problems go away,
but He will give you the power
to deal with and overcome them.

BILLY GRAHAM

I have told you these
things, so that in me
you may have peace.
In this world you
will have trouble.
But take heart! I have
overcome the world.

JOHN 16:33 NIV

I will lift up my eyes to the hills—
From whence comes my help?
My help comes from the LORD,
Who made heaven and earth....
The LORD shall preserve you
from all evil; He shall preserve
your soul. The LORD shall preserve
your going out and your coming in
From this time forth, and even
forevermore.

PSALM 121:1–2, 7–8 NKJV

> We have a Father in heaven who is almighty, who loves His children...and whose very joy and delight it is to... help them at all times.
>
> GEORGE MUELLER

*G*od guides us, despite our
uncertainties and our vagueness,
even through our failings and
mistakes.... He leads us step
by step, from event to event.
Only afterwards, as we look back
over the way we have come and
reconsider certain important
moments in our lives in the light
of all that has followed them, or
when we survey the whole progress
of our lives, do we experience the
feeling of having been led without
knowing it, the feeling that God
has mysteriously guided us.

PAUL TOURNIER

When we obey him,
every path he guides
us on is fragrant with
his lovingkindness
and his truth.

PSALM 25:10 TLB

*G*od...with a loving Father's heart, is always searching our heart.... And when we reach our heavenly home and read the records of life, we shall better know and appreciate the infinite love of that Divine Friend who has watched within as the Spirit of prayer and breathed out our every need to the heart of God.

A. B. SIMPSON

Can anything ever separate us from Christ's love? Does it mean he no longer loves us if we have trouble or calamity?... No, despite all these things, overwhelming victory is ours through Christ, who loved us.

ROMANS 8:35, 37 NIV

*B*lessed be the LORD, my rock...
he is my steadfast love and
my fortress, my stronghold and
my deliverer, my shield and he
in whom I take refuge.

PSALM 144:1–2 ESV

Let my soul take refuge...
beneath the shadow of
Your wings: let my heart,
this sea of restless waves,
find peace in You, O God.

AUGUSTINE

Why would God promise a refuge unless He knew we would need a place to hide once in a while?

NEVA COYLE

*G*rasp the fact that God is for you—let this certainty make its impact on you in relation to what you are up against at this very moment; and you will find in thus knowing God as your sovereign protector, irrevocably committed to you in the covenant of grace, both freedom from fear and new strength for the fight.

J. I. PACKER

*If God is for us,
who can be against us?*

ROMANS 8:31 NIV

*W*e are always in the presence of God.... There is never a nonsacred moment! His presence never diminishes. Our awareness of His presence may falter, but the reality of His presence never changes.

MAX LUCADO

God is everywhere.... And where God is, there is heaven—*heaven!* where His majesty reigns in glory.

TERESA OF AVILA

You have...one God and Father of all, who rules over all, works through all, and is present in all. Everything you are and think and do is permeated with Oneness.

EPHESIANS 4:6 MSG

The temptations in your life are no different from what others experience. And God is faithful. He will not allow the temptation to be more than you can stand. When you are tempted, he will show you a way out so that you can endure.

1 CORINTHIANS 10:13 NLT

Perhaps this moment is unclear.... Trust that God will help you work it out, and that all the unclear moments will bring you to that moment of clarity and action when you are known by Him and know Him.

WENDY MOORE

Lord Jesus Christ, You are the
sun that always rises, but never sets.
You are the source of all life, creating
and sustaining every living thing.
You are the source of all food,
material and spiritual, nourishing us
in both body and soul. You are the
light that dispels the clouds of error
and doubt. May I walk in Your light,
be nourished by Your food, be
sustained by Your mercy, and
be warmed by Your love.

ERASMUS

It is you who light my lamp; the LORD my God lightens my darkness.

PSALM 18:28 ESV

I'll take the hand of those who don't know the way, who can't see where they're going. I'll be a personal guide to them, directing them through unknown country. I'll be right there to show them what roads to take, make sure they don't fall into the ditch. These are the things I'll be doing for them—sticking with them, not leaving them for a minute.

ISAIAH 42:16 MSG

We do not understand the intricate pattern of the stars in their courses, but we know that He who created them does, and that just as surely as He guides them, He is charting a safe course for us.

BILLY GRAHAM

My Lord God, I have no idea where I am going. I do not see the road ahead of me. I cannot know for certain where it will end.... But I... trust You always though I may seem to be lost and in the shadow of death. I will not fear, for You are ever with me. And You will never leave me to face my perils alone.

THOMAS MERTON

Be assured, if you walk with Him and look to Him and expect help from Him, He will never fail you.

GEORGE MUELLER

et I am always with you; you hold me by my right hand.

PSALM 73:23 NIV

*God, who is our dwelling place,
is also our fortress. It can only mean
one thing, and that is, that if we will
but live in our dwelling place, we
shall be perfectly safe and secure
from every assault.*

HANNAH WHITALL SMITH

He who dwells in the
shelter of the Most High
will abide in the shadow
of the Almighty. I will
say to the Lord, "My refuge
and my fortress, my God,
in whom I trust."

PSALM 91:1–2 ESV

*I*t is right and good that we, for all things, at all times, and in all places, give thanks and praise to You, O God. We worship You, we confess to You, we praise You, we bless You, we sing to You, and we give thanks to You: Maker, Nourisher, Guardian, Healer, Lord, and Father of all.

LANCELOT ANDREWES

For Thine is the Kingdom, and the power and the glory, for ever. Amen.

MATTHEW 6:14[†]

In closing, give God the praise. Thank Him for what He is about to do, for the blessings He brings in answer to your prayers. Proclaim who He is and worship His mighty name.

*E*xpect unexpected things, "above all that we ask or think."... Worship God in His glory. Think of what He can do, and how He delights to hear the prayers of His redeemed people. Think of your place and privilege in Christ, and expect great things!

ANDREW MURRAY

Now to him who is able to do immeasurably more than all we ask or imagine, according to his power that is at work within us, to him be glory...for ever and ever! Amen.

EPHESIANS 3:20-21 NIV

How blessed all those in whom
you live, whose lives become roads
you travel; they wind through
lonesome valleys, come upon brooks,
discover cool springs and pools
brimming with rain! God-traveled,
these roads curve up the mountain,
and at the last turn—Zion!
God in full view!

PSALM 84:5–7 MSG

It is God to whom and with whom we travel, and while He is the End of our journey, He is also at every stopping place.

ELISABETH ELLIOT

Open wide the windows of our spirits and fill us full of light; open wide the door of our hearts that we may receive and entertain You with all the powers of our adoration.

CHRISTINA ROSSETTI

Many, O LORD my God, are the wonders which You have done, and Your thoughts toward us; there is none to compare with You.

PSALM 40:5 NASB

So you will go out with joy and be led out in peace. The mountains and hills will burst into song before you, and all the trees in the fields will clap their hands.... These things will be a reminder of the LORD's promise.

ISAIAH 55:12–13 NCV

*May your life become one
of glad and unending
praise to the Lord as you
journey through this
world, and in the world
that is to come!*

TERESA OF AVILA

When I look at the galaxies on a clear night—when I look at the incredible brilliance of creation, and think that this is what God is like, then instead of feeling intimidated and diminished by it, I am enlarged—I rejoice that I am part of it.

MADELEINE L'ENGLE

The heavens declare
the glory of God;
and the firmament
shows His handiwork.

PSALM 19:1 NKJV

Gratitude consists in a watchful, minute attention to the particulars of our state, and to the multitude of God's gifts, taken one by one. It fills us with a consciousness that God loves and cares for us, even to the least event and smallest need of life.

HENRY EDWARD MANNING

God is glorified not only by His glory being seen, but by its being rejoiced in.... His glory is then received by the whole soul.

JONATHAN EDWARDS

O LORD, our Lord, how majestic is your name in all the earth! You have set your glory above the heavens.... When I consider your heavens, the work of your fingers, the moon and the stars, which you have set in place, what is man that you are mindful of him, the son of man that you care for him? You made him a little lower than the heavenly beings and crowned him with glory and honor.... O LORD, our Lord, how majestic is your name in all the earth!

PSALM 8:1, 3–5, 9 NIV

I ask—ask the God of our Master, Jesus Christ, the God of glory—to make you intelligent and discerning in knowing him personally, your eyes focused and clear, so that you can see exactly what it is he is calling you to do, grasp the immensity of this glorious way of life he has for his followers, oh, the utter extravagance of his work in us who trust him— endless energy, boundless strength!

EPHESIANS 1:17–19 MSG

The end of prayer is that I come to know God Himself.

OSWALD CHAMBERS

*D*elight yourself in the LORD
and he will give you the desires of
your heart. Commit your way to
the LORD; trust in him and he
will do this: He will make your
righteousness shine like the dawn,
the justice of your cause like
the noonday sun.

PSALM 37:4–6 NIV§

Our fulfillment comes in
knowing God's glory,
loving Him for it, and
delighting in it.

God's pursuit of praise from us and our pursuit of pleasure in Him are one and the same pursuit. God's quest to be glorified and our quest to be satisfied reach their goal in this one experience: our delight in God which overflows in praise.

JOHN PIPER

FOR THINE IS THE KINGDOM, AND THE POWER
AND THE GLORY FOR EVER. AMEN.

The LORD bless you and keep you;
The LORD make His face shine
upon you, and be gracious to you;
The LORD lift up His countenance
upon you, and give you peace.

NUMBERS 6:24–26 NKJV

He is the King of kings, the radiance of God's glory, the Lord of the spaceless, fabulous, infinite universe; omniscient, omnipotent, omnipresent, unspeakably holy... and yet He condescended to be enclosed in human flesh.

23. Jenny Coulter
24. Beth Hunter
25. Alana Bell
26. Robyn Millar
27. Lucy Marks
28. Ellen Andrews
29. Leah McGilton
30. Georgia McMahon
31. Hannah-Rose Smith
32. Abbie Kirker
33. Grace Horner
34. William Adams
35. Nathaniel Plunkett

Little People

1. Vicki Allen
2. Clare Bankhead
3. Tim Purdue
4. Lucy Bankhead
5. Rachel Purdue
6. Carol Montgomery
7. Kathryn Comins
8. Ryan Comins
9. Daria McMaster
10. Dylan McMaster
11. Peter
12. Abi McQueen
13. Adam McQueen
14. Evan McVeigh
15. Steph Beck
16. Andrew Moore
17. Timothy Moore
18. Jacob Ogilby
19. Jude Ogilby
20. Emily Brannigan
21. Erin McConnell
22. Alexis McKernan

Thine, O LORD, is the greatness, and the power and the glory, and the victory and the majesty; for all that is in the heaven and in the earth is Thine. Thine is the kingdom, O LORD, and Thou art exalted as head above all. Both riches and honor come from Thee, and Thou reignest over all. And in Thine hand is power and might; and in Thine hand it is to make great, and to give strength unto all. Now therefore, our God, we thank Thee and praise Thy glorious name.

I CHRONICLES 29:11-13

Prayers

- Tim and Vicki
- Melissa McKibbin
- Rachel, Grace and Samuel
- Elenor
- Wider family circle
- Ross Patterson
- Youth Fellowship
- C of I
- PCN

My mouth is filled with Your praise and with Your glory all day long.

PSALM 71:7–8 NASB

Ellie Claire™ Gift & Paper Corp.
Minneapolis, MN 55337
www.ellieclaire.com

The Lord's Prayer

© 2012 by Ellie Claire™ Gift & Paper Corp.

ISBN 978-1-60936-604-9

Scripture quotations marked † are taken from the 21st Century King James Version®, copyright © 1994. Used by permission of Deuel Enterprises, Inc., Gary, SD 57237. All rights reserved.

Other Scripture references are from the following sources: The Holy Bible, New International Version®, NIV®. Copyright © 1973, 1978, 1984, 2011 by Biblica, Inc.™ Used by permission of Zondervan. All rights reserved worldwide. (Scripture quotation marked NIV§ is taken from the NIV® © 1984 version.) The New King James Version (NKJV). Copyright © 1982 by Thomas Nelson, Inc. Used by permission. The Holy Bible, English Standard Version® (ESV), copyright © 2001 by Crossway Bibles, a publishing ministry of Good News Publishers. Used by permission. The New American Standard Bible® (NASB), Copyright © 1960, 1962, 1963, 1968, 1971, 1972, 1973, 1975, 1977, 1995 by The Lockman Foundation. Used by permission. The Holy Bible, New Living Translation (NLT), copyright 1996, 2004, 2007 by Tyndale House Foundation. Used by permission of Tyndale House Publishers, Inc., Carol Stream, Illinois 60188. The Message (MSG). Copyright © 1993, 1994, 1995, 1996, 2000, 2001, 2002 by Eugene Peterson. Used by permission of NavPress, Colorado Springs, CO. The Living Bible (TLB) © 1971. Used by permission of Tyndale House Publishers, Inc., Carol Stream, Illinois 60188. The New Century Version® (NCV). Copyright © 1987, 1988, 1991, 2005 by Thomas Nelson, Inc. Used by permission. All rights reserved.

Excluding Scripture verses and deity pronouns, in some quotations references to men and masculine pronouns have been replaced with gender-neutral or feminine references. Additionally, in some quotations we have carefully updated verb forms and wording that may distract modern readers.

Stock or custom editions of Ellie Claire titles may be purchased in bulk for educational, business, ministry, fundraising, or sales promotional use. For information, please email specialmarkets@summersidepress.com.

Compiled by Barbara Farmer
Cover and interior design by Lisa and Jeff Franke

Printed in China